BONUS!

LOOK FOR THE CAMERA in our instructions and watch our technique videos made just for you! **www.LeisureArts.com/6383**

Formal Jewelry

Perfect for weddings, proms, and other parties, these elegant designs are extra easy to crochet. Each uses mostly chain stitches and basic jewelry techniques that are explained step by step. They're great for gifts, too!

LEISURE ARTS, INC. • Maumelle, Arkansas

CLASSIC PEARL NECKLACE

Finished Size: Approximately 68" (172.5 cm)

EASY

SHOPPING LIST

Thread

DMC Metallic pearl, size 5
[27.3 yards (25 meters) per skein]:

- ☐ Gold - 1 skein

Steel Crochet Hook

- ☐ Size 1 (2.75 mm)

Beads

8 mm Pearls

- ☐ White - 42
- ☐ Bead stop - 1

Additional Supplies

- ☐ Flexible wire beading needle
- ☐ Clear glue

Before beginning, see Basic Techniques, pages 26-32.

Model is wearing purchased earrings.

INSTRUCTIONS

Use the beading needle to put a bead stop on end of the thread *(Fig. 3c, page 29)*, leaving a 6" (15 cm) end, then string 42 pearls onto the thread *(Figs. 3a & b, page 29)*.

Strand

Leaving a 6" (15 cm) end, ch 5, ch around bead *(Figs. 1a-d, page 27)*, (ch 10, ch around bead) until all pearls are used, ch 5; join with slip st to first ch, finish off leaving a 6" (15 cm) end.

Place a small amount of glue on the joining slip st and allow to dry.

Thread the beading needle with one thread end and weave it into the chains.

Trim the end, then place a small amount of glue on it and allow to dry.

Repeat with the remaining end, weaving it into the chain in the opposite direction.

DOUBLE PEARL BRACELET

EASY

SHOPPING LIST

Thread

DMC Metallic pearl, size 5 [27.3 yards (25 meters) per skein]:

- ☐ Silver - 1 skein

Steel Crochet Hook

- ☐ Size 1 (2.75 mm)

Beads

8 mm Pearls

- ☐ White - 22{26}
- ☐ Bead stop - 1

Additional Supplies

- ☐ Flexible wire beading needle
- ☐ Small end cones - 2
- ☐ Small barrel-shaped magnetic clasp
- ☐ 2" (5 cm) Eye pins - 2
- ☐ Chain-nose pliers - 2 pair
- ☐ Round-nose pliers - 1 pair
- ☐ Wire cutters
- ☐ Clear glue

SIZE INFORMATION

Size: Small {Large}

Finished Size: Approximately 7½{8}"/19{20.5} cm long

Size Note: We have printed the instructions for the sizes in different colors to make it easier for you to find:

- Size Small in Blue
- Size Large in Pink

Instructions in Black apply to both sizes.

Before beginning, see Basic Techniques, pages 26-32.

Model is wearing purchased earrings.

INSTRUCTIONS

Use the beading needle to put a bead stop on the end of the thread *(Fig. 3c, page 29)*, leaving a 6" (15 cm) end, then string 22{26} pearls onto the thread *(Figs. 3a & b, page 29)*.

Strand (Make 2)

Leaving a 6" (15 cm) end, ch 4, ch around bead *(Figs. 1a-d, page 27)*, (ch 1, ch around bead) 10{12} times, ch 4; finish off leaving a 6" (15 cm) end: 11{13} pearls on **each** strand.

Finishing

See Sample on page 30 and refer to Finishing, pages 31 and 32.

Tie the strands together with an overhand knot at each end *(Fig. 4, page 29)*, placing the knot as close to the last chain as possible.

Place a small amount of glue on each knot, tighten each knot and allow to dry. Trim the ends to ¼" (7 mm).

Using the chain-nose pliers, open the end of one eye pin *(Fig. 5, page 31)*.

Slide the open end of the eye pin around the knot at one end of the strands; close the eye pin with the pliers.

Wrap the eye pin end tightly around the strands *(Figs. 6a & b, page 31)*.

Slide one end cone on the eye pin to cover the knot.

Make a loop on the end of the eye pin to attach the clasp *(Figs. 7a-c, page 32)*. Open the new loop to attach one side of the magnetic clasp.

Repeat at the opposite end of the bracelet.

TRIPLE PEARL NECKLACE

Finished Size: Approximately 16" (40.5 cm) long

EASY

SHOPPING LIST

Thread

DMC Metallic pearl, size 5
[27.3 yards (25 meters) per skein]:

- ☐ Silver - 1 skein

Steel Crochet Hook

- ☐ Size 1 (2.75 mm)

Beads

12 mm Pearls

- ☐ White - 78
- ☐ Bead stop - 1

Additional Supplies

- ☐ Flexible wire beading needle
- ☐ Large end cones - 2
- ☐ Large toggle clasp
- ☐ 2" (5 cm) Eye pins - 2
- ☐ Chain-nose pliers - 2 pair
- ☐ Round-nose pliers - 1 pair
- ☐ Wire cutters
- ☐ Clear glue

Before beginning, see Basic Techniques, pages 26-32.

Model is wearing purchased earrings.

INSTRUCTIONS

Use the beading needle to put a bead stop on the end of the thread *(Fig. 3c, page 29)*, leaving a 6" (15 cm) end, then string 78 pearls *(Figs. 3a & b, page 29)* onto the thread.

First Strand

Leaving a 6" (15 cm) end, ch 9, ch around bead *(Figs. 1a-d, page 27)*, (ch 2, ch around bead) 23 times, ch 9; finish off leaving a 6" (15 cm) end: 24 pearls on strand.

Second Strand

Leaving a 6" (15 cm) end, ch 9, ch around bead, (ch 2, ch around bead) 25 times, ch 9; finish off leaving a 6" (15 cm) end: 26 pearls on strand.

Third Strand

Leaving a 6" (15 cm) end, ch 9, ch around bead, (ch 2, ch around bead) 27 times, ch 9; finish off leaving a 6" (15 cm) end: 28 pearls on strand.

Finishing

See Sample on page 30 and refer to Finishing, pages 31 and 32.

Tie the strands together with an overhand knot at each end *(Fig. 4, page 29)*, placing the knot as close to the last chain as possible.

Place a small amount of glue on each knot, tighten each knot and allow to dry. Trim the ends to ¼" (7 mm).

Using the chain-nose pliers, open the end of one eye pin *(Fig. 5, page 31)*.

Slide the open end of the eye pin around the knot at one end of the strands; close the eye pin with the pliers.

Wrap the eye pin end tightly around the strands *(Figs. 6a & b, page 31)*.

Slide one end cone on the eye pin to cover the knot.

Make a loop on the end of the eye pin to attach the clasp *(Figs. 7a-c, page 32)*. Open the new loop to attach one side of the toggle clasp.

Repeat at the opposite end of the necklace.

DOUBLE PEARL NECKLACE

Finished Size: Approximately 16" (40.5 cm) long

EASY

SHOPPING LIST

Thread

DMC Metallic pearl, size 5
[27.3 yards (25 meters) per skein]:

- ☐ Silver - 1 skein

Steel Crochet Hook

- ☐ Size 1 (2.75 mm)

Beads

8 mm Pearls

- ☐ White - 59
- ☐ Bead stop - 1

Additional Supplies

- ☐ Flexible wire beading needle
- ☐ Large end cones - 2
- ☐ Large barrel-shaped magnetic clasp
- ☐ 2" (5 cm) Eye pins - 2
- ☐ Chain-nose pliers - 2 pair
- ☐ Round-nose pliers - 1 pair
- ☐ Wire cutters
- ☐ Clear glue

Before beginning, see Basic Techniques, pages 26-32.

Model is wearing purchased earrings.

INSTRUCTIONS

Use the beading needle to put a bead stop on the end of the thread *(Fig. 3c, page 29)*, leaving a 6" (15 cm) end, then string 59 pearls *(Figs. 3a & b, page 29)* onto the thread.

First Strand

Leaving a 6" (15 cm) end, ch 6, ch around bead *(Figs. 1a-d, page 27)*, (ch 1, ch around bead) 28 times, ch 6; finish off leaving a 6" (15 cm) end: 29 pearls on strand.

Second Strand

Leaving a 6" (15 cm) end, ch 6, ch around bead, (ch 1, ch around bead) 29 times, ch 6; finish off leaving a 6" (15 cm) end: 30 pearls on strand.

Finishing

See Sample on page 30 and refer to Finishing, pages 31 and 32.

Tie the strands together with an overhand knot *(Fig. 4, page 29)* at each end, placing the knot as close to the last chain as possible.

Place a small amount of glue on each knot, tighten each knot and allow to dry. Trim the ends to ¼" (7 mm).

Using the chain-nose pliers, open the end of one eye pin *(Fig. 5, page 31)*.

Slide the open end of the eye pin around the knot at one end of the strands; close the eye pin with the pliers.

Wrap the eye pin end tightly around the strands *(Figs. 6a & b, page 31)*.

Slide one end cone on the eye pin to cover the knot.

Make a loop on the end of the eye pin *(Figs. 7a-c, page 32)* to attach the clasp. Open the new loop to attach one side of the magnetic clasp.

Repeat at the opposite end of the necklace.

SPARKLE NECKLACE

Finished Size: Approximately 19" (48.5 cm) long, unstretched

EASY

SHOPPING LIST

Thread

Metallic elastic cord, size 0.5 mm [75 yards (68.5 meters) per package]:

- ☐ Silver - 1 package

Steel Crochet Hook

- ☐ Size 1 (2.75 mm)

Beads

Variety pack of beads

- ☐ Silver and grey - 176
- ☐ Bead stop - 1

Additional Supplies

- ☐ Flexible wire beading needle
- ☐ Toggle clasp
- ☐ Clear glue

Before beginning, see Basic Techniques, pages 26-32.

Model is wearing purchased earrings.

INSTRUCTIONS

Use the beading needle to put a bead stop on the end of the cord *(Fig. 3c, page 29)*, leaving a 10" (25.5 cm) end, then string all beads onto the cord, varying the size of the beads randomly.

Body

Leaving a 10" (25.5 cm) end for sewing, ch 113.

Row 1: Sc in second ch from hook and in each ch across, randomly working sc with bead 44 times *(Figs. 2a-d, page 28)*: 112 sc.

Rows 2-4: Ch 1, turn; sc in each sc across randomly working sc with bead 44 times.

Row 5: Ch 1, turn; sc in each sc across; finish off.

Finishing

Thread the beading needle with long end. Using the long end, sew through the loop at one end of the toggle clasp several times, then weave the end into the stitches, reversing directions several times.

With beading needle and cord, sew remaining end of clasp to opposite end of necklace in same manner.

Cut the cords close to the work. Place a small amount of glue on the ends and allow to dry.

Repeat at the opposite end of the necklace.

TRIPLE PEARL BRACELET

Finished Size: Approximately 7½" (19 cm) long

EASY

SHOPPING LIST

Thread

DMC Metallic pearl, size 5
[27.3 yards (25 meters) per skein]:

- ☐ Silver - 1 skein

Steel Crochet Hook

- ☐ Size 1 (2.75 mm)

Beads

8 mm Pearls

- ☐ Pink - 18
- ☐ Bead stop - 1

Additional Supplies

- ☐ Flexible wire beading needle
- ☐ Small end cones - 2
- ☐ Lobster claw clasp with jump ring
- ☐ 2" (5 cm) Eye pins - 2
- ☐ Chain-nose pliers - 2 pair
- ☐ Round-nose pliers - 1 pair
- ☐ Wire cutters
- ☐ Clear glue

Before beginning, see Basic Techniques, pages 26-32.

INSTRUCTIONS

Use the beading needle to put a bead stop on the end of the thread *(Fig. 3c, page 29)*, leaving a 6" (15 cm) end, then string 18 pearls onto the thread *(Figs. 3a & b, page 29)*.

Strand (Make 3)

Leaving a 6" (15 cm) end, ch 6, ch around bead *(Figs. 1a-d, page 27)*, (ch 4, ch around bead) 5 times, ch 6; finish off leaving a 6" (15 cm) end: 6 pearls on **each** strand.

Finishing

See Sample on page 30 and refer to Finishing, pages 31 and 32.

Tie the strands together with an overhand knot at each end *(Fig. 4, page 29)*, placing the knot as close to the last chain as possible.

Place a small amount of glue on each knot, tighten each knot and allow to dry. Trim the ends to ¼" (7 mm).

Using the chain-nose pliers, open the end of one eye pin *(Fig. 5, page 31)*.

Slide open end of the eye pin around the knot at one end of the strands; close the eye pin with the pliers.

Wrap the eye pin end tightly around the strands *(Figs. 6a & b, page 31)*.

Slide one end cone on the eye pin to cover the knot.

Make a loop on the end of the eye pin *(Figs. 7a-c, page 32)* to attach the clasp. Open the new loop to attach the jump ring of the clasp.

Repeat at the opposite end of the bracelet.

SILVER BAREFOOT SANDAL

EASY

SHOPPING LIST

Thread

Metallic elastic cord, size 0.5 mm [75 yards (68.5 meters) per package]:

- ☐ Silver - 1 package

Steel Crochet Hook

- ☐ Size 1 (2.75 mm)

Beads

6 mm Faceted beads

- ☐ Clear - 38{50}
- ☐ Bead stop - 1

Additional Supplies

- ☐ Flexible wire beading needle
- ☐ Clear glue

SIZE INFORMATION

Size: Small {Large}

Finished Length: Approximately 7{8}"/18{20.5} cm (unstretched)

Size Note: We have printed the instructions for the sizes in different colors to make it easier for you to find:

- Size Small in Blue
- Size Large in Pink

Instructions in Black apply to both sizes.

Before beginning, see Basic Techniques, pages 26-32.

INSTRUCTIONS

Sandal (Make 2)

Use the beading needle to put a bead stop on the end of the cord *(Fig. 3c, page 29)*, leaving a 6" (15 cm) end, then string 19{25} beads *(Figs. 3a & b, page 29)* onto the cord.

ANKLE

Rnd 1: Leaving a 6" (15 cm) end, ch 4, ch around bead *(Figs. 1a-d, page 27)*, (ch 9, ch around bead) 4{5} times, ch 5; being careful **not** to twist ch, join with slip st to form a ring: 50{60} chs.

INSTEP AND TOE RING

Rnd 1: Ch 35{45}, being careful **not** to twist ch, slip st in 16{20}th ch from hook (Toe Ring); do **not** turn, sc in same ch as slip st just made and in next 3 chs, sc with bead *(Figs. 2a-d, page 28)* in next ch, (sc in next 2 chs, sc with bead in next ch) 4{6} times, sc in next 3 chs, slip st in same ch on Ankle as last slip st: 20{26} sc.

Rnd 2: Ch 1, turn; sc in first 20{26} sc across Instep; sc in next 15{19} chs on Toe Ring; slip st in same ch on Instep as last slip st: 35{45} sc.

Rnd 3: Ch 1, turn; sc in first 19{23} sc, sc with bead in next sc, (sc in next 2 sc, sc with bead in next sc) 4{6} times, sc in next 3 sc; working in Ankle chs, sc in next 9 chs, (sc with bead in next ch, sc in next 9 chs) 4{5} times; slip st in last ch; finish off leaving a 6" (15 cm) end.

Thread beading needle with one cord end; weave the end into the stitches, reversing direction several times.

Cut the cord close to the work. Place a small amount of glue on the end and allow to dry.

Repeat with the remaining cord end.

SOMETHING BLUE GARTER

Finished Size: Approximately 12" (30.5 cm) circumference, unstretched

EASY

SHOPPING LIST

Thread

Metallic elastic cord, size 0.5 mm [75 yards (68.5 meters) per package]:

- ☐ Silver - 1 package

Steel Crochet Hook

- ☐ Size 1 (2.75 mm)

Beads

Size 6 Glass beads, silver-lined,

- ☐ Clear and Aqua mix - 84
- ☐ Bead stop - 1

Additional Supplies

- ☐ Flexible wire beading needle
- ☐ Clear glue

Before beginning, see Basic Techniques, pages 26-32.

INSTRUCTIONS

Body

Leaving a 6" (15 cm) end, ch 85.

Row 1: Sc in second ch from hook and in each ch across: 84 sc.

Rows 2-6: Ch 1, turn; sc in each sc across; do **not** finish off.

Seam

Ch 1, do **not** turn; place short edges of Garter together, working through **both** layers, slip st in end of each row across; finish off leaving a 6" (15 cm) end.

Thread beading needle with one long end and weave through sts at seam until end is secure.

Cut the cord close to the work. Place a small amount of glue on the end and allow to dry.

Repeat with remaining cord end.

The seam indicates the **wrong** side of the Garter.

Beaded Edging

Use beading needle to put a bead stop *(Fig. 3c, page 29)* on the end of the cord leaving a 6" (15 cm) end, then string 84 beads *(Figs. 3a & b, page 29)* onto the cord in random color order.

FIRST SIDE

Place a slip knot on the hook.

Rnd 1: With **wrong** side facing and working in sc on Row 6, join cord with a sc as follows: Insert hook in same st as seam, YO and pull up a loop (2 loops on hook), YO and draw through **both** loops on hook *(Fig. A)*, sc complete *(Fig. B)*.

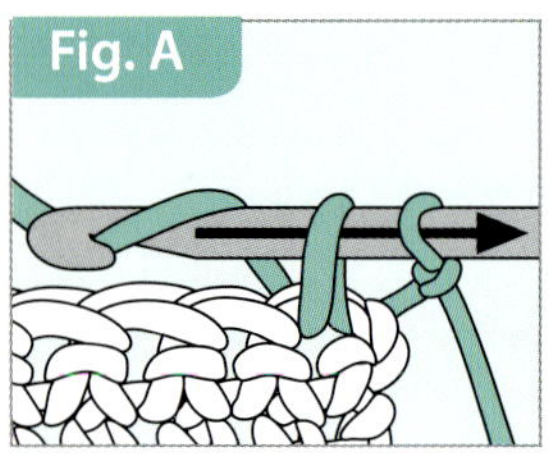
Fig. A

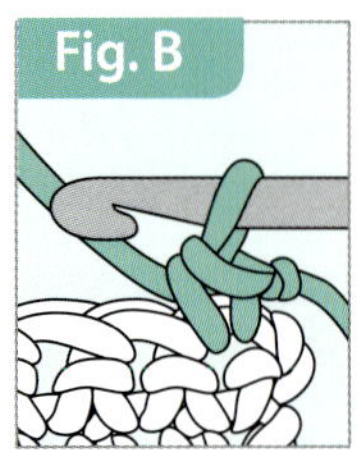
Fig. B

Sc with bead in next st *(Figs. 2a-d, page 28)*, (sc in next st, sc with bead in next st) around; join with slip st to first sc, finish off leaving a 6" (15 cm) end.

SECOND SIDE

Rnd 1: With **wrong** side of Garter facing and working in free loops of beginning chain *(Fig. C)*, work same as First Side.

Fig. C

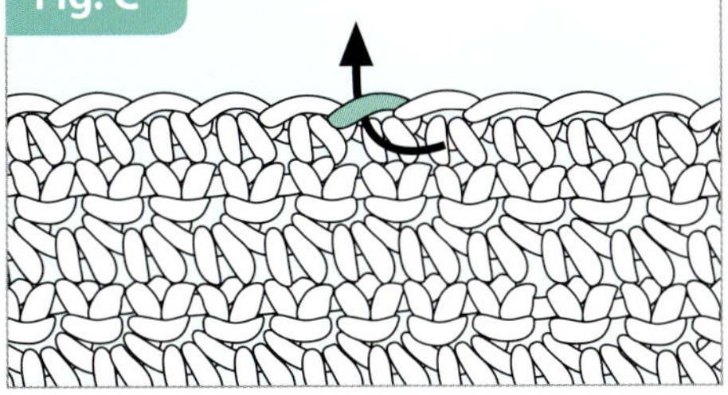

Hide the remaining cord ends, placing a small amount of glue on each end and allowing to dry.

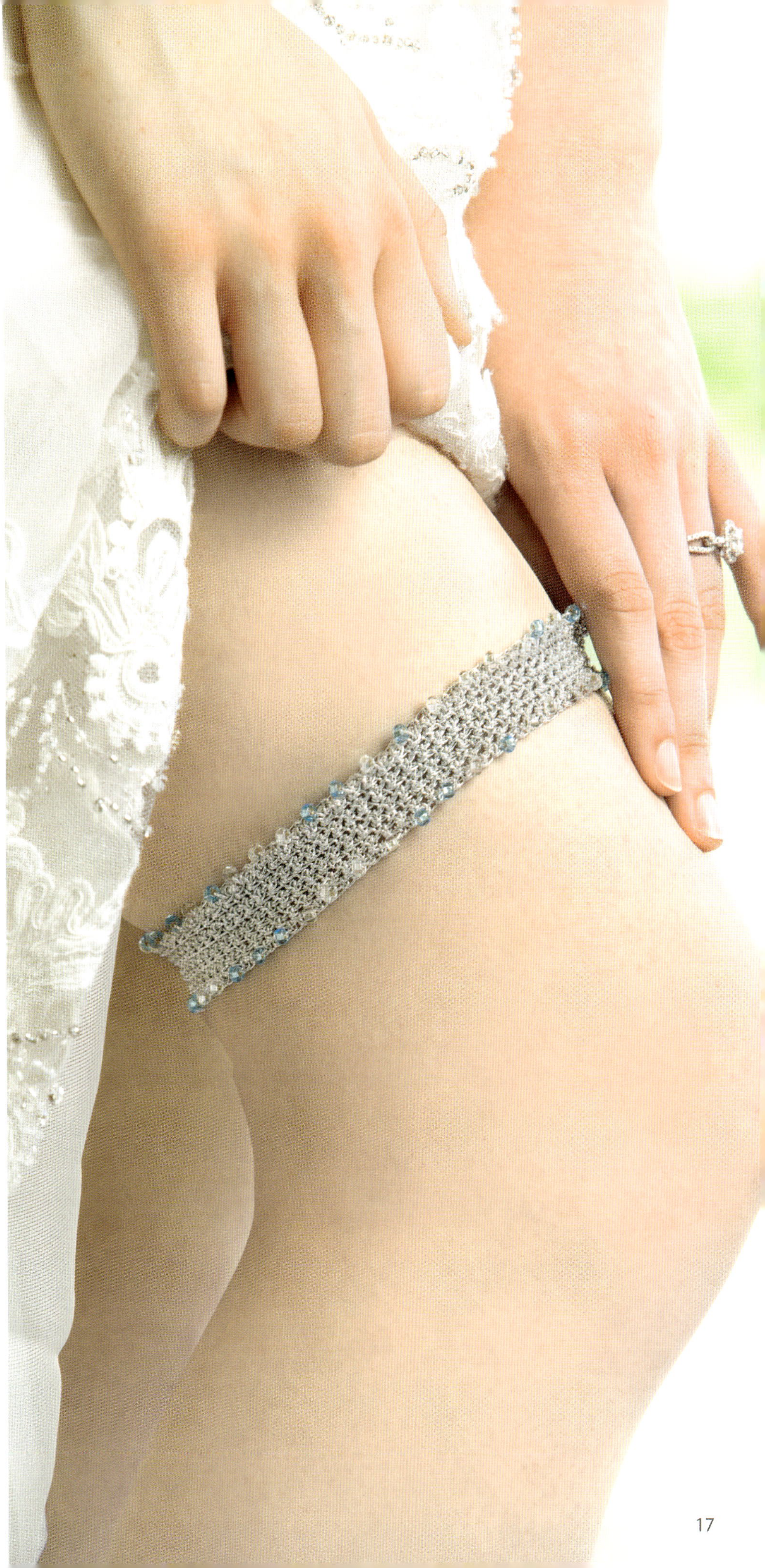

FORMAL HEADBAND

Finished Size: Approximately 17" (43 cm) circumference, unstretched

EASY

SHOPPING LIST

Thread

Metallic elastic cord, size 0.5 mm [75 yards (68.5 meters) per package]:

- ☐ Silver - 1 package

Steel Crochet Hook

- ☐ Size 1 (2.75 mm)

Beads

Size 6 mm Faceted beads

- ☐ Silver - 22
- ☐ Bead stop - 1

Additional Supplies

- ☐ Flexible wire beading needle
- ☐ Clear glue

Before beginning, see Basic Techniques, pages 26-32.

Model is wearing purchased earrings.

INSTRUCTIONS

Body

Use the beading needle to put a bead stop on the end of the cord *(Fig. 3c, page 29)*, leaving a 6" (15 cm) end, then string 22 beads onto the cord *(Figs. 3a & b, page 29)*.

Leaving a 6" (15 cm) end, ch 119.

Row 1 (Right side)**:** Sc in second ch from hook and in each ch across: 118 sc.

Row 2: Ch 1, turn; sc in first 5 sc, sc with bead in next sc *(Figs. 2a-d, page 28)*, (sc in next 10 sc, sc with bead in next sc) across to last 2 sc, sc in last 2 sc: 11 sc with beads.

Row 3: Ch 1, turn; sc in each sc across.

Row 4: Ch 1, turn; sc in first 8 sc, (sc with bead in next sc, sc in next 10 sc) across: 11 sc with beads.

Row 5: Ch 1, turn; sc in each sc across; do **not** finish off.

Seam

Ch 1; place short edges of Headband together, working through **both** layers, slip st in end of each row across; finish off leaving a 6" (15 cm) end.

Thread the beading needle with one long end and weave through the sts at the seam until the end is secure.

Cut the cord close to the work. Place a small amount of glue on the end and allow to dry.

Repeat with the remaining cord end.

FLOATING PEARL NECKLACE

Finished Size: Approximately 18" (45.5 cm) long

EASY

SHOPPING LIST

Thread

DMC Metallic pearl, size 5
[27.3 yards (25 meters) per skein]:

- ☐ Silver - 1 ball

Steel Crochet Hook

- ☐ Size 1 (2.75 mm)

Beads

8 mm Pearls

- ☐ Pink - 21
- ☐ Bead stop - 1

Additional Supplies

- ☐ Flexible wire beading needle
- ☐ Small end cones - 2
- ☐ Large barrel-shaped magnetic clasp
- ☐ 2" (5 cm) Eye pins - 2
- ☐ Chain-nose pliers - 2 pair
- ☐ Round-nose pliers - 1 pair
- ☐ Wire cutters
- ☐ Clear glue

Before beginning, see Basic Techniques, pages 26-32.

INSTRUCTIONS

Use the beading needle to put a bead stop on end of thread *(Fig. 3c, page 29)*, leaving a 6" (15 cm) end, then string 21 pearls onto thread *(Figs. 3a & b, page 29)*.

Strand

Leaving a 6" (15 cm) end, ch 3, ch around bead *(Figs. 1a-d, page 27)*, ch 3, (ch around bead, ch 3) until all pearls are used; finish off leaving a 6" (15 cm) end.

Finishing

See Sample on page 30 and refer to Finishing, pages 31 and 32.

Tie an overhand knot at each end *(Fig. 4, page 29)*, placing the knot as close to the last chain as possible.

Place a small amount of glue on each knot, tighten each knot and allow to dry. Trim the ends to ¼" (7 mm).

Using the chain-nose pliers, open the end of one eye pin *(Fig. 5, page 31)*.

Slide the open end of the eye pin around the knot at one end of the necklace; close the eye pin with the pliers.

Wrap the eye pin end tightly around the chain *(Figs. 6a & b, page 31)*.

Slide one end cone on the eye pin to cover the knot.

Make a loop on the end of the eye pin to attach the clasp *(Figs. 7a-c, page 32)*. Open the new loop to attach one side of the magnetic clasp.

Repeat at the opposite end of the necklace.

BLACK BAREFOOT SANDAL

Finished Size: Approximately 8" (20.5 cm) long, unstretched

EASY

SHOPPING LIST

Thread

Elastic cord, size 0.5 mm
[75 yards (68.5 meters)
per package]:

- ☐ Black - 1 package

Steel Crochet Hook

- ☐ Size 1 (2.75 mm)

Charm

1" (2.5 cm) Connector-style charm (with a loop on opposing ends)

- ☐ 2

Additional Supplies

- ☐ Clear glue
- ☐ Tapestry needle

Before beginning, see Basic Techniques, pages 26-32.

INSTRUCTIONS

Sandal (Make 2)

INSTEP

Toe Ring: Leaving a 6" (15 cm) end, ch 18; being careful **not** to twist ch, join with slip st to form a ring.

Rnd 1: Ch 1, sc in each ch around; join with slip st to first sc: 18 sc.

Begin working in rows.

Row 1: Ch 1, turn; sc in first 3 sc, leave remaining 15 sc unworked: 3 sc.

Row 2: Ch 1, turn; 2 sc in first sc, sc in next sc, 2 sc in last sc: 5 sc.

Row 3: Ch 1, turn; 2 sc in first sc, sc in next 3 sc, 2 sc in last sc: 7 sc.

Row 4: Ch 1, turn; 2 sc in first sc, sc in next 5 sc, 2 sc in last sc: 9 sc.

Rows 5-21: Ch 1, turn; sc in each sc across.

Row 22: Ch 1, turn; sc in first 4 sc, pull loop on hook to be very long, remove loop from hook, with **wrong** side of one charm facing, slip loop through one end of charm *(Fig. A)*, place loop back on hook and tighten, sc in last 5 sc.

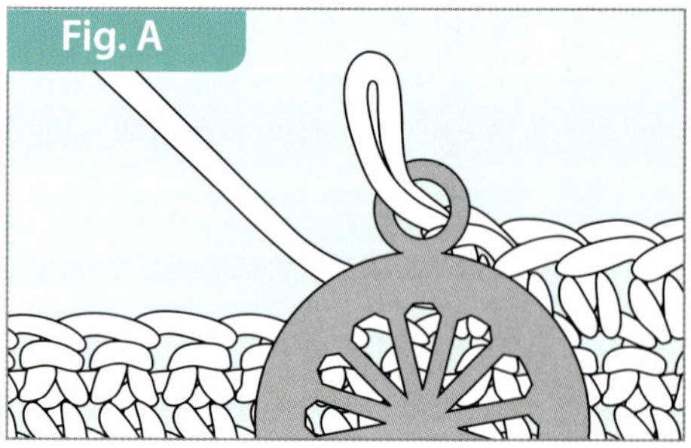

Fig. A

Rows 23-31: Ch 1, turn; sc in each sc across.

Row 32: Ch 1, turn; sc in first 4 sc, pull loop on hook to be very long, remove loop from hook, with **right** side of attached charm facing, slip loop through charm's remaining end, place loop back on hook and tighten, sc in last 5 sc.

Rows 33-47: Ch 1, turn; sc in each sc across; do **not** finish off.

ANKLE

Rnd 1: Ch 39, turn; being careful **not** to twist ch, sc in each sc and in each ch around; join with slip st to first sc, finish off leaving a 6" (15 cm) end.

Thread the tapestry needle with one long end; weave the end into the stitches, reversing direction several times.

Cut the cord close to the work. Place a small amount of glue on the end and allow to dry completely.

Repeat with the remaining cord end.

BLACK ON BLACK NECKLACE

Finished Size: Approximately 38" (96.5 cm) long

EASY

SHOPPING LIST

Thread

DMC Pearl cotton, size 8
[87 yards (79.5 meters) per ball]:

- ☐ Black - 1 ball

Steel Crochet Hook

- ☐ Size 1 (2.75 mm)

Beads

6 mm pearls

- ☐ Grey - 54
- ☐ Bead stop - 1

Additional Supplies

- ☐ Flexible wire beading needle
- ☐ Small end cones - 2
- ☐ Large barrel-shaped magnetic clasp
- ☐ 2" (5 cm) Eye pins - 2
- ☐ Chain-nose pliers - 2 pair
- ☐ Round-nose pliers - 1 pair
- ☐ Wire cutters
- ☐ Clear glue

Before beginning, see Basic Techniques, pages 26-32.

INSTRUCTIONS

Use the beading needle to put a bead stop on the end of the thread *(Fig. 3c, page 29)*, leaving a 6" (15 cm) end, then string 54 pearls *(Figs. 3a & b, page 29)* onto the thread.

Strand

Leaving a 6" (15 cm) end, ch 8, ch around bead *(Figs. 1a-d, page 27)*, (ch 2, ch around bead) until all pearls have been used, ch 8; finish off leaving a 6" (15 cm) end.

Finishing

See Sample on page 30 and refer to Finishing, pages 31 and 32.

Tie an overhand knot at each end *(Fig. 4, page 29)*, placing the knot as close to the last chain as possible.

Place a small amount of glue on each knot, tighten each knot and allow to dry. Trim ends to ¼" (7 mm).

Using the chain-nose pliers, open end of one eye pin *(Fig. 5, page 31)*.

Slide the open end of the eye pin around the knot at one end; close the eye pin with the pliers.

Wrap the eye pin end tightly around the chain *(Figs. 6a & b, page 31)*.

Slide one end cone on the eye pin to cover the knot.

Make a loop on the end of the eye pin to attach the clasp *(Figs. 7a-c, page 32)*. Open the new loop to attach one side of the magnetic clasp.

Repeat at the opposite end of the necklace.

BASIC TECHNIQUES

ABBREVIATIONS

ch(s)	chain(s)
cm	centimeters
mm	millimeters
Rnd(s)	Round(s)
sc	single crochet(s)
st(s)	stitch(es)
YO	yarn over

SYMBOLS & TERMS

( ) or **[ ]** — work enclosed instructions **as many** times as specified by the number immediately following **or** contains explanatory remarks.

colon (:) — the numbers given after a colon at the end of a row or round denotes the number of stitches you should have on that row or round.

GAUGE

Gauge is not of great importance with the projects in this book. When working with elastic cord, work **loosely** in order to allow the project to have full range of stretchiness.

CROCHET TERMINOLOGY		
UNITED STATES		INTERNATIONAL
slip stitch (slip st)	=	single crochet (sc)
single crochet (sc)	=	double crochet (dc)
half double crochet (hdc)	=	half treble crochet (htr)
double crochet (dc)	=	treble crochet(tr)
treble crochet (tr)	=	double treble crochet (dtr)
double treble crochet (dtr)	=	triple treble crochet (ttr)
triple treble crochet (tr tr)	=	quadruple treble crochet (qtr)
skip	=	miss

BEGINNER	Projects for first-time crocheters using basic stitches. Minimal shaping.
EASY	Projects using yarn with basic stitches, repetitive stitch patterns, simple color changes, and simple shaping and finishing.
INTERMEDIATE	Projects using a variety of techniques, such as basic lace patterns or color patterns, mid-level shaping and finishing.
EXPERIENCED	Projects with intricate stitch patterns, techniques and dimension, such as non-repeating patterns, multi-color techniques, fine threads, small hooks, detailed shaping and refined finishing.

STEEL CROCHET HOOKS																
U.S.	00	0	1	2	3	4	5	6	7	8	9	10	11	12	13	14
Metric - mm	3.5	3.25	2.75	2.25	2.1	2	1.9	1.8	1.65	1.5	1.4	1.3	1.1	1	.85	.75

CROCHET BASICS

To Work A Chain Around A Bead

Slide a bead up against the last chain made *(Fig. 1a)*.

Pull the loop on the hook larger to fit around the bead *(Fig. 1b)*, then YO *(Fig. 1c)* and draw through the loop on the hook to complete the chain *(Fig. 1d)*.

Fig. 1a

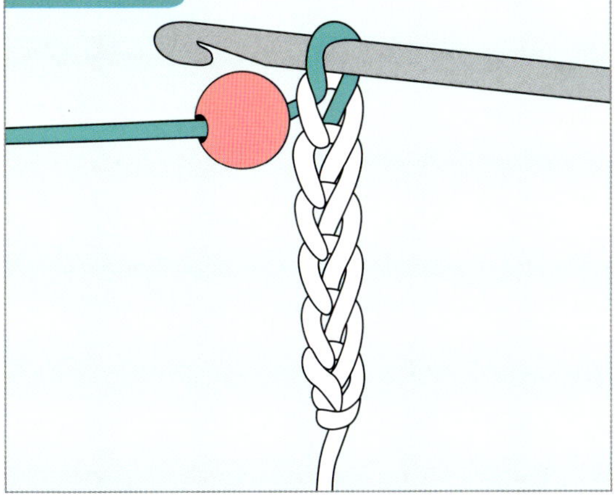

Fig. 1b

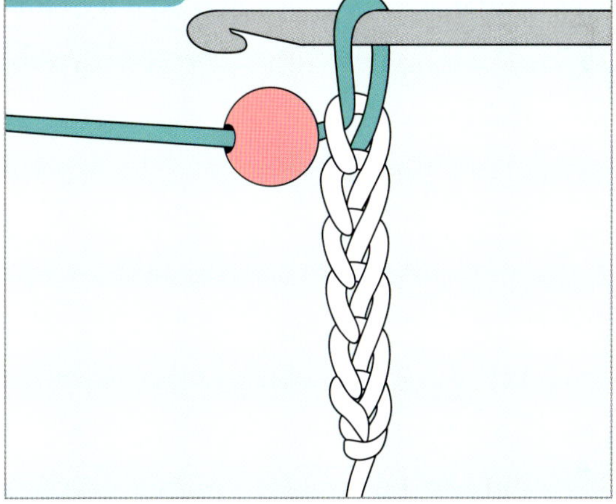

Fig. 1c

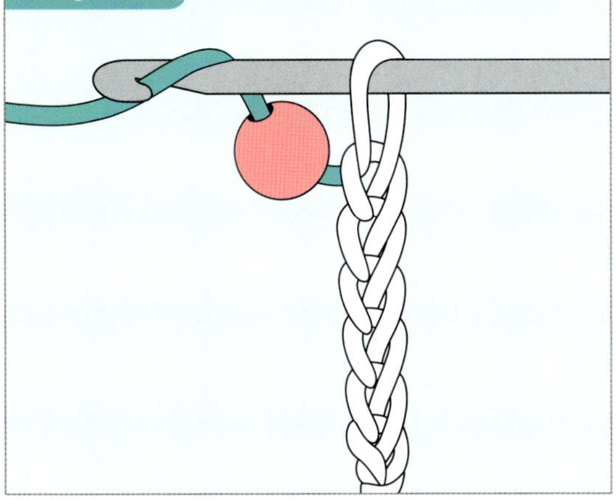

Fig. 1d

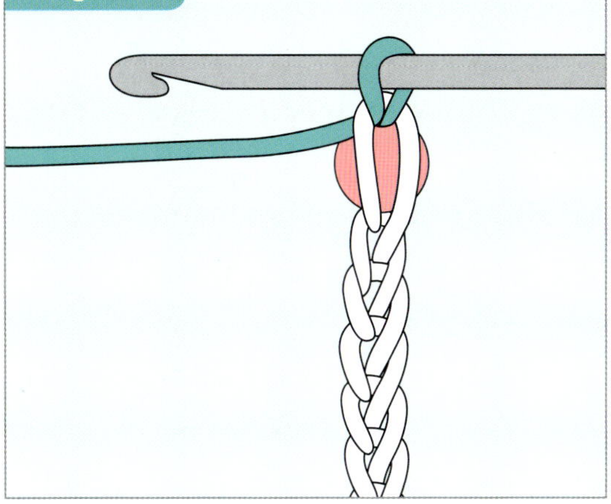

Single Crochet With A Bead *(abbreviated sc with bead)*

Slide a bead up against the last stitch made *(Fig. 2a)*. Insert the hook in the next stitch, YO and pull up a loop, YO and draw through both loops on hook *(Fig. 2b)* single crochet completed *(Fig. 2c)*. The bead will be to the **back** of the stitch *(Fig. 2d)*.

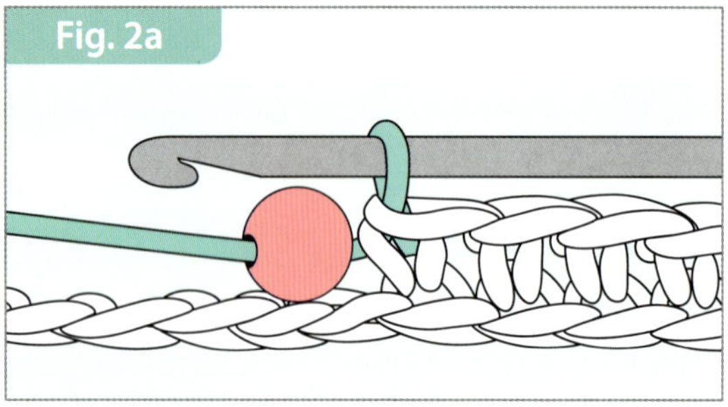
Fig. 2a

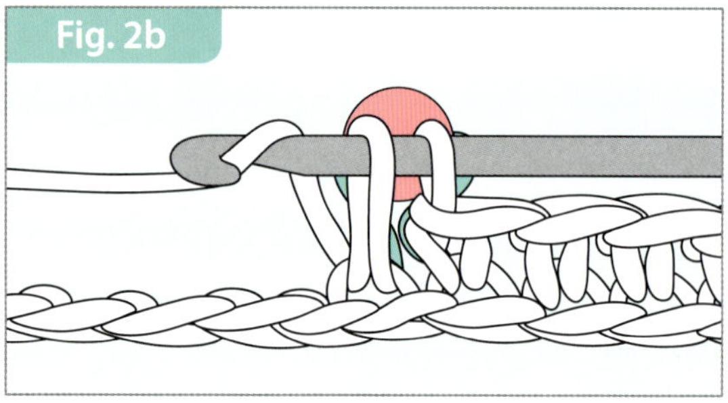
Fig. 2b

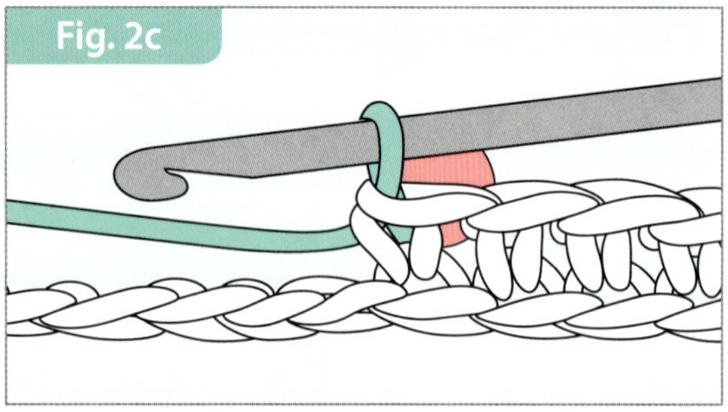
Fig. 2c

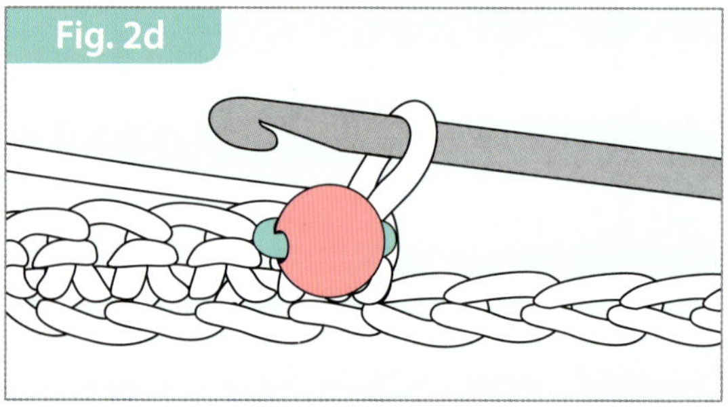
Fig. 2d

MEET THE DESIGNER

A crocheter for many years, Karen McKenna enjoys creating designs to fill practical needs. She came up with her jewelry designs while experimenting with beads and alternate crochet materials. Usually her favorite projects are gloves, mitts, and mittens.

Karen's designs have appeared in national magazines and yarn industry publications. For more about Karen, see her blog at ihookdesign.blogspot.com.

The New Jersey native and longtime resident of the Pacific Northwest is now retired and living in Florida. She and her husband have traveled the world and visited every state except North Dakota. Karen also loves to read mysteries and political thrillers and to make long-distance bike rides.

JEWELRY BASICS

Stringing Pearls/Beads

Thread a flexible wire beading needle with the cord or thread *(Figs. 3a & b)*, then string the number of beads or pearls needed for each pattern onto the cord or thread, beginning with a bead stop, if needed.

Fig. 3a

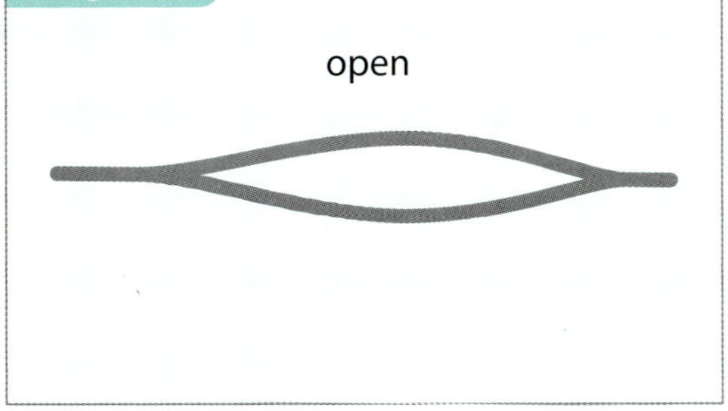

Fig. 3b

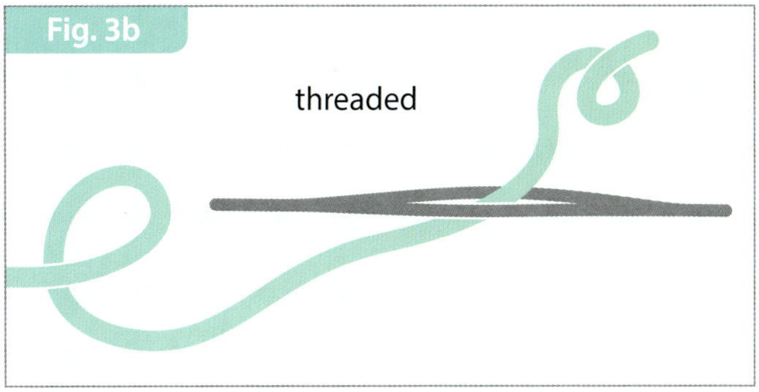

Using a Bead Stop

When working with a cut length of thread or cord, you don't want to be concerned that the beads will slide off the other end. A bead stop does just that: it stops the beads from sliding off your thread.

You can simply use any extra bead you may have on hand. Before you start stringing your beads, thread on a bead stop. Run the thread around the bead and pass it through the bead again, securing it in place *(Fig. 3c)*.

When you are ready to finish off your crochet, the bead stop can removed by loosening the thread around it and slipping it off.

Fig. 3c

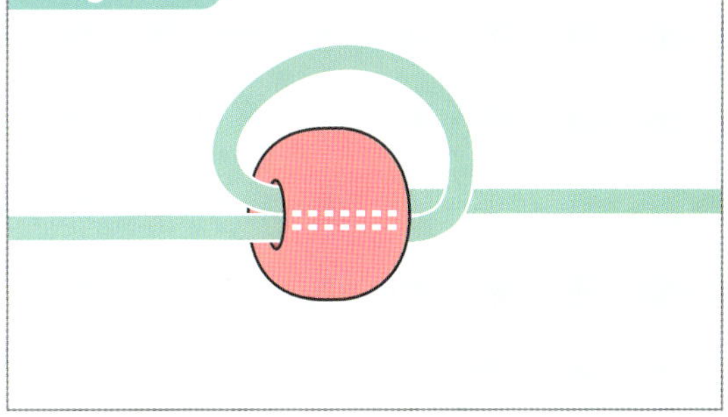

Overhand Knot

Tie an overhand knot to join crocheted strands *(Fig. 4)*.

Fig. 4

Components

All components used in this book can be found in the beading/jewelry section of any craft store. Here are products similiar to the ones we used.

End cones are findings that hide the ends of multi-strand jewelry pieces.

An eye pin is a straight wire with a loop on one end which can be opened and closed using chain-nose pliers.

Clasps of all sizes, shapes and styles are available. **Lobster clasps (A)** are shaped like a lobster claw and have a spring-action closure. **A toggle clasp** (B) is secured by sliding the bar through the loop. Magnetic clasps (C) used in this book are cylindrical or barrel shaped in different sizes.

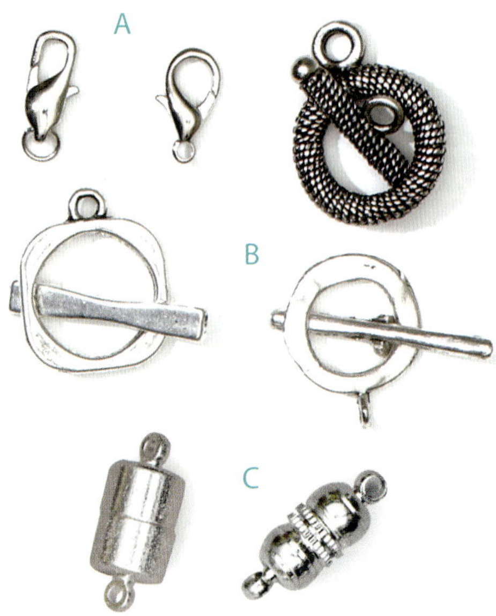

FINISHING

Opening and Closing an Eye Pin

To open an eye pin properly, hold each side of the eye with a pair of chain-nose pliers. Open the loop by pulling one pair of pliers toward you while pushing the other pair away *(Fig. 5)*.

Close the loop by pushing and pulling the pliers in the opposite direction, bringing the eye back together.

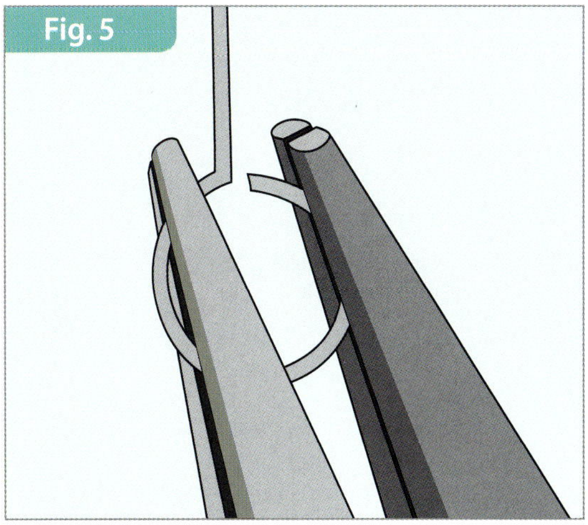

Fig. 5

Using Eye Pins to Secure Crochet Chains

Open the eye pin and close it around the overhand knot *(see Opening and Closing An Eye Pin)*.

Tightly wrap the eye pin around the strands *(Fig. 6a)*.

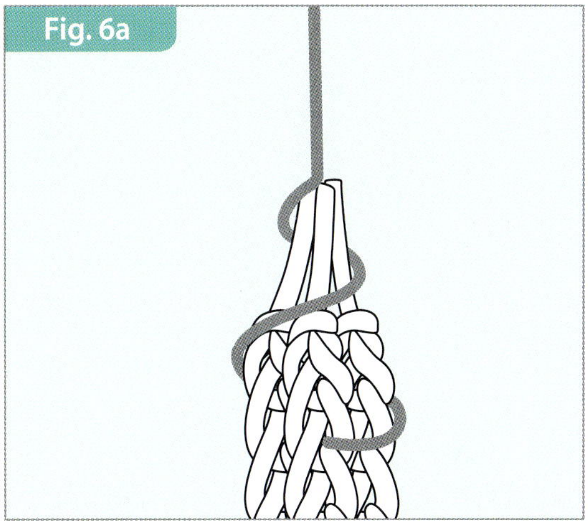

Fig. 6a

Thread the eye pin end through a cone and pull until the wrapped ends are drawn into the cone *(Fig. 6b)*.

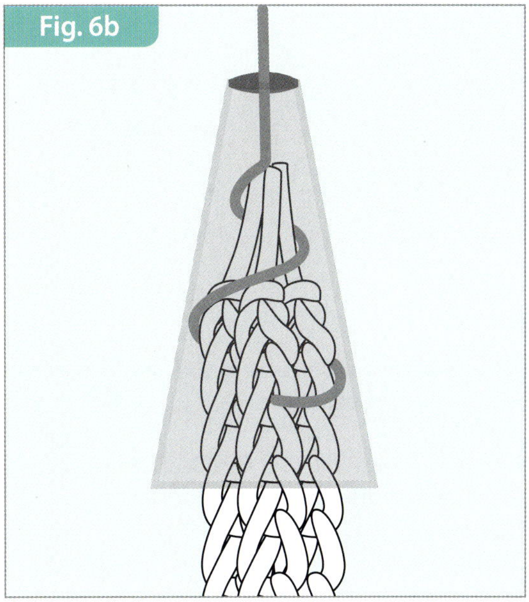

Fig. 6b

Making a Loop with an Eye Pin

Leaving about ½" (12 mm), cut off the excess wire. Using the chain-nose pliers, bend the wire at a 90˚ angle *(Fig. 7a)*. Grasp the wire end with the round-nose pliers. Turn the pliers and bend the wire into a loop *(Figs. 7b & c)*. Release the pliers. Straighten or twist the loop further, if necessary.

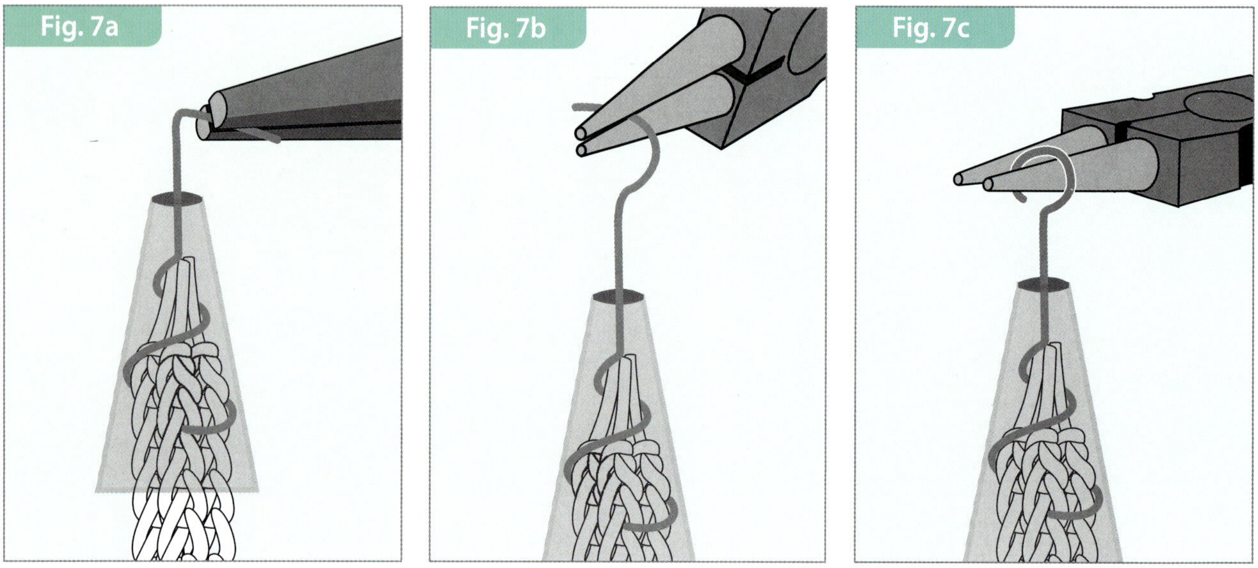

Open and close this loop with two pair of chain-nose pliers to attach to clasps or jump rings *(see Opening and Closing An Eye Pin, page 31)*.

We've created bonus videos for you @ www.leisurearts.com/6383

Take a look!

Production Team: Writer/Instructional Editor - Sarah J. Green; Editorial Writer - Susan Frantz Wiles; Senior Graphic Artist - Lora Puls; Graphic Artist - Jessica Bramlet; Photo Stylist - Lori Wenger; and Photographers - Jason Masters and Ken West.